TO:

FROM:

The
10
Golden Rules of
Customer
Service

& the Story of the $6,000 Egg

TODD DUNCAN and DEB DUNCAN

Internal images © page viii, Squaredpixels/Getty Images; page xi, 24,
Jose Luis Pelaez Inc/Getty Images; page xvi, Marianna Massey/Getty
Images; page xxvi, Al Qayyum Yahya/EyeEm/Getty Images; page 12,
Klaus Vedfelt/Getty Images; page 32, Thomas Barwick/Getty Images;
page 40, Jetta Productions/Getty Images; page 64, Tom Merton/
Getty Images; page 72, PeopleImages/Getty Images; page 74, Juan
Lin/EyeEm/Getty Images; pages 76, 92, 94, Hero Images/Getty
Images; page 78, izusek/Getty Images; page 80, Alistair Berg/Getty
Images; pages 82, 88, Maskot/Getty Images
Internal images on pages 14, 15, 16, 46, 52, 91, 98 have been provided
by the authors.
Internal images on pages xii, xviii, xxii, 2, 4, 8, 10, 16, 18, 20, 26, 30,
34, 38, 42, 44, 48, 54, 56, 58, 61, 62, 70, 84, 86 have been provided
by Pexels and Pixabay; these images are licensed under CC0 Creative
Commons and have been released by the author for public use.

Published by Simple Truths, an imprint of Sourcebooks, Inc.
P.O. Box 4410, Naperville, Illinois 60567-4410
(630) 961-3900
Fax: (630) 9612168
sourcebooks.com

Printed and bound in China.
OGP 10 9 8 7 6 5 4 3 2 1

To businesses and their teams
around the globe—may the
impact you make change the lives
of your customers every time!
No exception. No excuses.

Contents

Introduction:

The $6,000 Egg

ONE SATURDAY, MY wife, Deb, and I headed out to our favorite restaurant for an early lunch. It's a chic Newport Beach research and development test kitchen that experiments with new menu items before putting them in their well-known chain of restaurants.

Their food and ambience are spectacularly perfect, and for more than two years, and during one hundred visits, the experience and service were always exceptional. In fact, the servers joked that Deb and I should have our name etched in the bar stools because we always sat in the same two spots, had a leisurely lunch, and watched sports. That was our idea of the perfect Saturday. We liked to call it a "two-hour vacation."

They have an incredible cheeseburger. And we figured that if we went to the gym first and worked out, we were allowed to indulge and split the cheeseburger.

That particular day, we'd already each had an appetizer and drinks when a new server came by to take our entrée order. She described the day's special—a buttermilk and bacon waffle with Vermont maple syrup, topped with a sunny-side up egg. It sounded decadent, but I had already worked out and had my heart set on the cheeseburger.

My wife loves to have a fried egg on top of her burger, so in an attempt to be nominated as husband of the year, I asked if they could add an egg. Being Scottish, I also asked how much it would cost. The server said, "Two bucks, but I'm not sure the kitchen can do it."

After checking, she said, "The kitchen can't add the egg. They are too busy."

The restaurant had just opened, and the kitchen was making sunny-side up eggs for the waffles. But when someone tells me something isn't possible, and my wife is involved, I don't give up easily. I waited a

few minutes and ordered the same thing with another server who knows us well. He grimaced. "Let me see if the kitchen can do it." Same answer: "They are too busy and aren't prepared to do anything that isn't on the menu." We didn't get it.

I smiled and asked if I could speak to the manager, Natalie. The minute she arrived, you could tell she was ready for a battle. No smile. No positive gestures. Just a simple "I understand you have a problem?"

I explained that I simply wanted a side order of an egg. She said, "We can't do that."

"Why?" I asked.

"We only order a certain number of eggs per day, and we have to save them for our special waffle. If we don't have the egg, we can't sell one of our most popular dishes."

"So you can't do it?"

"Nope," she said.

"So let me make sure we are tracking here. I spend at least $6,000 a year at your restaurant, and I have one simple request for a $2 egg for my burger. You are telling me you can't make that happen, because you only order enough eggs for your waffle dish?"

"Yes."

"So a one-time visitor who orders a waffle for $15

is more important to you than a $6,000 customer who comes in at least four to six times a month, but for whom you can't figure out how to get an egg?"

"We have to be able to serve the dishes we advertise, and we usually run out of the special ones. If we run out of eggs, we can't serve the waffle."

"As a manager, wouldn't you rather be one egg short and throw away a waffle that probably costs you fifty cents to make than throw away a loyal customer who brings you $6,000 a year?"

"It's our policy."

How sad she didn't have the authority to grant an egg. It was clear to me at that point that the manager—and perhaps the whole restaurant—had no clue about the value of a customer. But she could still save the situation, if she wanted.

I said, "You know what I would do if I were you? I'd send a busboy two hundred feet to the grocery store next door and buy half a dozen eggs. That might cost you a couple of bucks. You wouldn't have to throw away a waffle, I'd have an egg, and you would make me one happy customer."

"I can't do that," she responded.

I laughed. "In the time we've spent arguing about this, someone could have been there and back."

I could not believe what happened next. Natalie said, "I'm happy to take care of your bill for your inconvenience."

"That's stupid." She looked at me, dazed and confused. "You would rather spend your company's money to pay for my $75 tab than figure out how to get me a $2 egg?" I looked her squarely in the eyes and said, **"We are never coming back. This egg just cost you $6,000."**

We left immediately. For fun, we went next door to Whole Foods Market, the natural and organic grocery store, to check the price of eggs. We found them for thirty-three cents. Then, to our surprise, we stumbled upon a restaurant in the back of the store called Back Bay Tavern. We shared our experience with Sandee,

their server. She shook her head and told us that their company creed is **"We don't say no here."**

We looked over their menu and asked if we could create our own pizza, a combination not on their menu. She picked up her pen, smiled, and said, "We don't say no." We got creative and ordered a bacon, cheese, garlic, and olive oil pizza, with a sunny-side up egg on top. It was amazing!

Sandee told our story to several other employees who gathered around and talked about how great it is to work in such a customer-centric environment. **At this restaurant, employees are empowered to do whatever a customer requests.** They need not place a phone call or get an approval from a manager. That's empowered service.

It's absurd that any business owner can think for a moment that customers don't have other options. There are more than five hundred restaurants we can choose to eat at where we live. Why would the company that owns the research and development

restaurant, as well as three others in our zip code, ever allow a service breakdown, especially over an egg?

This is what is wrong with businesses today. They don't understand the changing dynamics of how consumers are spending their money. There is a new day in the service world. It's not coming—it's here! Today, the only way a business can survive is by following the 10 Golden Rules of Customer Service.

The company that knows how to *acquire*, optimize, and *retain* a customer the best gets paid the most, *period*!

We had gone to the research and development restaurant for two years, and that loyalty was canceled after one exceptionally bad experience. **Customers are lost as a result of an unsolved service breakdown, and they will share their story with everyone.** To date, over 400,000 people have heard this story.

IF YOU RUN A BUSINESS OR A DEPARTMENT:

Are your employees and teammates trained and empowered to make intelligent choices about taking care of customers during a breakdown?

Isn't it wiser to throw away a fifty-cent waffle, give the customer a two-dollar egg, and not pay for a seventy-five-dollar tab? All of this should make fiscal sense for a business.

Something is wrong with the service culture if a simple request is impossible.

> ▸ Are you ready for a game changer? What if Natalie had walked up to us and said, "I understand you are having a less than awesome experience. I will do whatever it takes to change that immediately"?

If she had done that, we would have been there every weekend, and she would have saved two valuable customers. No one should ever lose a client over an egg—or any other stupid service decision.

That is what this book is about. Not just good service, not just great service, but exceptional, off-the-charts service. The kind that doesn't just **WOW** customers—it blows their minds.

The rules have changed. Today, the options customers have to get what they want are so plentiful that not a single company or representative of that

company can afford to be powerless in the competitive world of service.

That's why the 10 Golden Rules of Customer Service are so essential. Collectively, they can change the destiny of your company and create an indelible legacy. They can change your life! And, as is so often the case, service generally gets down to the question **"How would you like to be treated?"** You want your customers shouting from the rooftops, **"More customer service! More! More!"**

GOLDEN RULE
in Action

◇◇◇◇◇◇◇◇◇◇

If the customer comes first, there is a
good chance the customer will come back.

◇◇◇◇◇◇◇◇◇◇

The
10

Golden Rules of
Customer
Service

NO.

1

Go Beyond and Beyond and Beyond

DENVER INTERNATIONAL AIRPORT is huge. You can get your shoes shined in about twenty different locations throughout the airport. On a recent trip, I arrived at my gate early for my flight home and decided I needed a shine. In Terminal B, I met a gentleman whose service set him apart. He shook my hand firmly and said, "Hi, my name is Alex. I'm a professional shoe shiner." How cool is that? He emanated deep pride for the experience he was about to provide. I'd **never** heard a shoe shiner brand himself in that way.

In more than twenty years of flying, Alex asked what no other shoe shine professional ever had: "Are you in a rush?" It was clear he had a plan. I told him I was not in a hurry. I had a feeling this was going to be a very different experience.

Alex began the shine. I was busy checking some

business emails and didn't really notice the time until I realized I had been seated for more than ten minutes. I never had a shine last that long. I looked down at my shoes—the laces had been pulled out, the leather flaps had been pulled back, and Alex had a Q-tip in his hands, cleaning out the crevices between the shoe and my lace flaps. I had **never** had this done before.

I was in the middle of reading an email from a friend when I heard a pair of clippers cutting off the frayed loose threads from sewing the shoe to the sole. I had **never** had this done either. I looked down a few minutes later, and he was using his fingers to bury the wax in the shoes. Most shoe shiners use a cloth. Alex caught me looking and said, **"The shine is better when you use only your fingers because the oil in your skin brings the shine alive."** *Seriously?* That was another first for me.

Another five minutes went by, and Alex announced, "All done." I looked down at my shoes and all I could say was **"Wow."** Then I looked at my watch. Alex had

"**Always give people more than they expect to get.**"

—NELSON BOSWELL

just spent twenty minutes on my shoes! I **never** had a twenty-minute shoe shine. And my shoes looked better than new.

I looked around for his posted prices, but there was no sign. That was another first. I'm used to paying eight to ten bucks for a shine, and they usually take eight to ten minutes. I guess that's a buck a minute.

I simply asked, "How much?" He looked at me with sense of joy and used the most incredible service line I have ever heard. He said, **"Whatever you think it's worth."** Are you kidding me? This shoe shine professional knew his value. He was working straight commission and continued adding more value at every opportunity.

I gave Alex thirty dollars. I had **never** paid that much for a shoe shine. That might sound crazy, but he earned every penny. Those shoes stayed shiny twice as long as any shine I'd ever received. By delivering a level of superior service, **Alex received an extra ten dollars beyond the going rate by going way, way beyond.**

I go back to Alex every time I'm in the Denver airport. I've told this story to thousands of people, and more than fifty of my friends and clients have sought out Alex as a result.

He knew the first Golden Rule of Customer Service—**Going Beyond and Beyond and Beyond.**

That's how to keep people coming back for more.

What would you get paid if your take-home pay was based on what your clients think your service was worth?

TEACHING MOMENT

When you think you have done enough, do more! When you think you are done, go a little bit further.

GOLDEN RULE
in Action

◇◇◇◇◇◇◇◇◇◇

The most effective and inexpensive advertising is a happy customer who tells the world about you, your product, and your company.

◇◇◇◇◇◇◇◇◇◇

NO.

2

Delight the Customer Every Step of the Way

A SOUTHERN CALIFORNIA Italian restaurant called Mama D's is packed every night of the week. In fact, their service and food quality are so legendary that if you are not there by 5:30 p.m., you will have a forty-five minute wait.

Being in such high demand, they have perfected the wait for a table, making it not only painless, but also delightful. **There is an art to creating a joyful journey during each step of the experience.**

On our first visit, we arrived early with our two teenage boys to avoid the wait. We all groaned when we learned we were not early enough and there would be a thirty-minute wait for a table. We moved outside to a curbside patio. It was a hot day, and we stood out there questioning if we were going to stay when

a waiter came out with a tray and asked if we'd like to sample their rolls. The rolls were piping hot, dripping with butter and garlic. Suddenly, with free appetizers, waiting for a table seemed less painful.

After we cleared the rolls off the young man's tray, he asked if he could bring us anything to drink. I joked, "Yeah, I'd love a cold beer." To which the young man said, "How cold would you like it?"

I've never been asked before how cold I'd like my beer, so I said, "Really cold." In less than five minutes, I had a beer in its own individual custom ice bucket. That's cold! It was just one indicator of how focused this restaurant is on its customers. Their attention to detail is simply spectacular.

If that was not enough, once we were seated and started reading the menu, our server asked us if we'd like to sample the "sausage of the day."

For the customer, that offer means more free snacks, while the restaurant is subtly "selling" one of its main dishes.

Mama D's philosophy reflects their mission statement, which is painted in large letters on the wall, as if it were a famous piece of art.

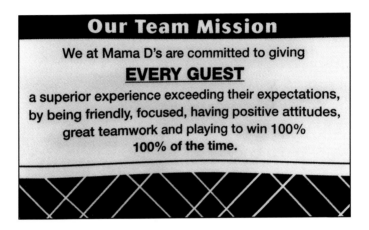

Our superior experience continued throughout the meal. We ordered two appetizers. After they arrived, the server asked how they were. One was excellent, the other not our favorite. In response, the server quickly pulled a free appetizer coupon out of his apron for our next visit. Brilliant! It was an immediate solution with a hook to entice us to come back again.

On another occasion, we needed a to-go bag for our food but forgot it after the meal. It was my son's favorite dish, so we called the restaurant to explain. The hostess said, "No problem. I will write your name down, and the next time you are in, we will

make a full order of that to take home." That's service at its best!

It gets even better. Deb's father once ordered a Diet Coke, but for whatever reason, they were out. The server said, "Don't worry. I will have it for you in less than three minutes." There happened to be a grocery store across the street, and without blinking an eye, the server bought a Diet Coke and had it back in a glass before you could count to one hundred!

TEACHING MOMENT

In what ways can you make your customers' experiences more gratifying and delightful?

GOLDEN RULE
in Action

◇◇◇◇◇◇◇◇◇◇

If you want business to get better for you, you have to get better at business.

◇◇◇◇◇◇◇◇◇◇

GOLDEN RULE

NO.

3

Make the Milestones
Magical and Memorable

DEB AND I were hurrying from the airport to our home. We'd had a busy tour, and we were ready to take a breather and relax. It was 3:00 p.m. Pacific time, and my phone chirped with an alarm. I looked down and saw the reminder on my calendar to call John Symond, the founder and chief executive officer of Aussie Home Loans. It was 9:00 a.m. in Sydney where John lives. And, as is always the case, he answered with his normal happy and enthusiastic voice, "Hey, mate!" And with all the joy and passion I could muster, I said, "It's that time of year. I wanted to call and wish you a happy birthday." His response was gratifyingly simple as he said, "You are unbelievable, Todd. You are the only person who calls me every year! Without fail! Nineteen years in a row, if I'm not mistaken. Thank you!"

Milestones should be magical and memorable. The important thing to remember is they must be systematic. Without the system, it's unlikely that this Golden Rule can be pulled off.

Let me explain.

I learned in May 1996 that John's birthday was August 17. Because Australia is across the international date line, I did a quick calculation and determined that to wish him a happy birthday, I needed to call him on August 16 from California. Since I wanted to be one of the first calls he got on his special day, I used the time difference calculator and learned that 3:00 p.m. in California was 9:00 a.m. his time, the next day. I logged this information into my calendar, set it up to recur every year, alarmed it, and set the start and end date for a total of forty years. I did this one time, and now every year, I have not failed to make the call. He's blown away! On the most recent call, he said, "I look forward every year to your call." Milestones are hugely valuable, especially when they are marked with an actual call. No Facebook. No emails. No card in the mail. But instead a good, old-fashioned phone call. At last count, I make more than three hundred calls a year just on birthdays.

The smart business adds this powerful strategy to its service model. Business owners and their employees decide how to make milestones memorable—how to make them magical, how to bring them to life, and how to make them indelible. In the end, the consumer experience is made more spectacular when the milestones are recognized and when they are designed to add value, acknowledge events, and create positive emotion. Milestones create the ultimate client connection.

"Customer service shouldn't just be a department, it should be the entire company."

—TONY HSIEH

Here's another example of a business that uses milestones to deepen the customer relationship. We have purchased cars from Thomas for more than fifteen years. He recognizes that keeping a client is more important than getting one. So, in each of those years, Thomas has managed milestones to perfection, making them magical and memorable.

Here are just some of the ways he does that:

▶ **Birthday call to me**

▶ **Birthday call to Deb**

▶ **Wedding anniversary text**

▶ **A call twenty-four hours after a service appointment to make sure we are happy**

▶ **A picture of prototype cars three or four years down the line to whet our appetite for our next purchase**

▶ **New Year's card**

Here's another example. Dr. Jones is our dentist. But he definitely sees his practice as a business. Because of that, he sees the real and differentiated opportunities to use milestones as ways to delight the customer. Here are a few things he does to make us feel special...about a dentist.

▶ **Cleaning reminders one month out from our next cleaning**

▶ **Twenty-four-hour confirmation calls prior to a procedure**

▶ **A personal phone call the night we had a procedure to check in and make sure all is well**

▶ **Birthday call**

How about your business? How can you make your customers' milestones come alive? What unique and special things can you do to create magical and memorable moments?

TEACHING MOMENT

Communicate consistently in very special ways, and your clients will love you and buy from you forever.

GOLDEN RULE
in Action

◇◇◇◇◇◇◇◇◇◇◇

If you want your customers for life, you
need to talk to them during their lives.

◇◇◇◇◇◇◇◇◇◇◇

GOLDEN RULE

NO.

4

Serve!

HER NAME WAS Mona. It was a Sunday, and Deb and I were leaving for the Caribbean the following morning to host our Achieving Leadership Excellence program at the Four Seasons Resort on the island of Nevis. But before we left, I needed to pick up a couple of new pairs of casual slacks. We went over to Nordstrom after church.

Upon our arrival, the salesperson, Mona, introduced herself and immediately asked what our needs

were. I told her, and the three of us went to the men's department, where, with Mona's guidance, we found a couple of pairs of pants for me to try on. They fit great, except the hems were unfinished, as is usually the case for someone of my height, being six-foot-five. It was 11:30 a.m., and we were leaving the following day at 6:00 a.m. Out of concern, I asked, "How soon could I get these hemmed?" She replied, "How soon would you like them?" I confessed that we were leaving early the following morning and told her we would need them that same day. She made a quick phone call to the tailor and assured me that wouldn't be a problem. "They will be done by 5:00 p.m.," she confirmed, to my delight. Then, without missing a beat, she said, **"Todd, you're probably going to be very busy packing for your trip, so rather than coming back here, why don't I deliver them to your home by 5:00 p.m.?** Would that be okay?"

"Wow, you will do that?" I replied, surprised.

"Absolutely," she assured.

With Mona's assurance, we were out the door without a worry. She had relieved our stress and made doing business easy.

Later that day, we were in our bedroom packing our suitcases when Mona arrived with the slacks—an hour early!

"I'm pretty confident these will fit perfectly," she said, "but just in case, why don't you try them on? The tailors are available until 9:00 p.m. if they don't fit."

They were a perfect fit, as I knew they would be. I gave Mona the thumbs-up and thanked her for her incredible service. As I walked her outside, I noticed an SL-Class Mercedes convertible in our driveway.

I asked Mona, "Is that yours?"

"Yes," she answered.

"You must be very successful," I said.

"Yes, by doing for all my clients what I just did for you."

"Todd," she continued, "you are going to buy from me for the rest of your life. Your family is also going to buy from me. And that's very important to me. **I want you to know that if we have it at Nordstrom, you can get it through me. I am your gateway to three floors of shopping excellence.** And even if we don't have it, I will still get it for you."

I understood why Mona is in the Million Dollar Club, which means she sells more than $1,000,000 of Nordstrom merchandise each year.

As we walked around the back of her car, I noticed her license plate frame read: *SERVE*. I also noticed that hanging in the back of her car were five more deliveries for other clients that day—Sunday. I knew she was right. My wife and I would never again buy from anyone at Nordstrom but Mona. We are her clients for life.

And it gets even better.

When we returned from our trip, we got a note from Mona in the mail:

Todd, I know you asked me if your slacks were going to go on sale and I told you no. Well, they did. Please find attached a credit to your Nordstrom account in the amount of $110. That is the difference between what you paid and the sales price.

—Mona

P.S. Looking forward to your next visit!!!!!!

TEACHING MOMENT
Overpromise, and then overdeliver.

GOLDEN RULE
in Action

◇◇◇◇◇◇◇◇◇◇◇

Most people will use your service once.
The key is to get them to use your
service forever.

◇◇◇◇◇◇◇◇◇◇◇

Use Over-the-Top Communication to *WOW* the Customer

THE MONTAGE RESORT is a beautiful hotel in Laguna Beach. It is a wonderful property and is, without question, one of the best providers of off-the-charts service we have ever experienced. One of the things we are most impressed with is how different departments communicate with each other. Every time we go there, we are surprised by something they do that is simply not expected. Here's one example of many:

For Deb's birthday, I called to make a reservation

at the hotel's restaurant, The Loft, and they did what every great restaurant should do. They asked, "Are you celebrating a special day?" I'm surprised how many places don't do that. I said, "Yes, it's my wife's birthday."

The day arrived, and, as always, the valet team greeted us. These guys are amazing. We don't know how they do it, but the valet guy said on our arrival, "How are the Duncans? It's great to see you again." With that, we were off to the hotel entrance and the experience began.

If you don't make a great first impression, all you can do next is try to make a great second impression.

We entered the restaurant, and as we arrived, the hostess asked our name, and without a moment of hesitation, she said, "Happy birthday, Mrs. Duncan." Do you know how good that makes people feel? We were seated outside where we watched a magnificent sunset and shared a decadent dinner.

As the evening drew to a close, magic started to

happen behind the scenes—the magic of interdepartmental communication. Once we paid the bill, without our knowledge, the server called the valet team and said, "The Duncans are done. Have their car brought up. And by the way, it's Mrs. Duncan's birthday." If nothing else happened, that would be world-class service, but the next department goes to work on delivering over-the-top service.

As we arrived back at the valet, our car was there. The valet opened Deb's door, and as she got in the car, we saw their special attention to detail. On the

dashboard were two Montage baseball caps, in blue and pink. Below the caps, perched on the console, was a card that said "Happy Birthday." We were blown away!

What a phenomenal demonstration of integrated communication! Everybody, at every level and department, plays a role in surprising the customer. It isn't a surprise then that on our anniversary, we got into the car and in the cup holders were two splits of Veuve Clicquot champagne and a "Happy Anniversary" card from the valet team! Talk about over-the-top service.

These guys rock!

TEACHING MOMENT

When there are multiple departments in an organization, how they communicate with one another can create a moment of magic for the customer. What can you do to make every handoff flawless and super memorable?

~ HAPPY BIRTHDAY ~

~KEITH Montross~

FUN FACTS
ABOUT APRIL 16

- THE ROLLING STONE
  DEBUT ALBUM
  "THE ROLLING STONES"
  WAS RELEASED!

- 1940 PRES ROOSEVELT
  THREW THE FIRST PITCH FOR
  A NEW BASEBALL SEASON!
  WITH A WILD PITCH HE
  HIT AND BROKE A CAMERA
  BELONGING TO A WASHINGTON
  POST REPORTER!

- CHINA SENT PRESIDE[NT]
  NIXON TWO GIANT PA[NDAS]
  AS A GIFT THIS DAY IN
  1972

- WILBUR WRIGHT WAS
  BORN ON THIS DAY IN
  1867

Edward P. Jean III

HAPPY BIRTHDAY !! :)

WE HOPE YOU HAD AN OUTSTANDING
TIME HERE AT MONTAGE! WE ARE
EXTREMELY THANKFUL YOU CHOOSE
TO SPEND PART OF YOUR SPECIAL
DAY HERE WITH US! HOPE TO
SEE YOU BACK SOON!
        SINCERELY-
        THE VALET TEAM!

GOLDEN RULE
in Action

⬥⬥⬥⬥⬥⬥⬥⬥⬥

The law of the encore: the greater the
performance, the louder the applause.

⬥⬥⬥⬥⬥⬥⬥⬥⬥

GOLDEN RULE

NO.

6

Deliver the Unexpected to Create Business Karma

by Deb Duncan

YEARS AGO, BEFORE we were married, I had a few minutes between afternoon meetings. I was starving and decided to grab an order of fries from In-N-Out Burger, a very popular drive-through burger chain with a location on Walnut Street in Pasadena. The line of cars in the drive-through line was crazy long. There was no way I could wait in line and still be on time. There were no parking spots available in the lot, and multiple cars were waiting for spots to open.

I noticed that there was no line at the walk-up window and the curb happened to be painted red as a "No Parking" zone. I parked illegally, zipped over to the window, and hustled back with my fries.

As I returned, a policeman was standing next to my car, writing a ticket. "I am sorry, officer," I said. "I goofed. I apologize." The drive-through employees were all looking out, watching while I asked, "Would it matter if I told you I was only parked here a minute?" He smiled, ripped the ticket out of his book, handed it to me, and drove away.

A fifty-four-dollar ticket made those the most expensive fries in the history of mankind. As I opened the car door, the manager who had seen the whole thing walked up and said, "Please let me pay the ticket for you." **Wow!** I said, "That's very kind of you, but all I bought was an order of fries. You don't make fifty-four dollars on me in a year." I didn't accept his offer, but the gesture was over-the-top and I never forgot it.

After Todd proposed, he asked me what I wanted to serve at our wedding reception. I quickly said, "In-N-Out Burgers!" So for our reception, at the beautiful Balboa Bay Club in Newport Beach, a seventy-five-foot mobile In-N-Out Burger cookout trailer was parked in front of the grand ballroom entrance to supply burgers for our guests.

Throughout the appetizer service and dinner and long after the cake was served, trays of hot cheeseburgers were being walked-in fresh off the truck with In-N-Out-clad servers. Our youngest son, Matt, ate four.

By the end of the evening, 750 burgers were served before the truck finally ran out of hamburger patties. Little did that Pasadena manager know his customer service gesture would come back many times over and create business karma for his brand.

When you take care of customers, they will be loyal forever. We call it the "10X Factor"—give ten times what you want to receive in either perceived or real value. It is the key to client retention, referrals, and brand lock-in. **What would it look like if you gave ten times more than you received in every business meeting? What would happen if you gave ten times more value than you get in your relationships?** When you play at level ten, the ROI (return on investment) is enormous.

Here's how it worked in this example. The In-N-Out

manager's gesture was worth 54X. Fries are one dollar. He offered to pay a fifty-four-dollar ticket. Years later, the **Business Karma Principle** kicked in and In-N-Out received nearly $5,000 because we hired them for our wedding. That would have been a 92X returned on the fifty-four-dollar ticket had the manager paid it! And just for making that offer, there was an actual ROI of 5,000X!

This was one manager who understood the Golden Rules of Customer Service! And an ROI of 5,000X!

TEACHING MOMENT

Every decision to add value to the customer expands value to the brand. How can you add the 10X Factor to your business?

BUSINESS KARMA

What goes around comes around!

GOLDEN RULE
in Action

◇◇◇◇◇◇◇◇◇◇

Give your best to your best so you can get the rest of what they have to give you.

◇◇◇◇◇◇◇◇◇◇

GOLDEN RULE

NO.

7

Blow Your Customer Away

ONE OF THE greatest days of my life was when I proposed to Deb, the love of my life. Full of passion, excitement, hopes, and dreams, I was, to say the least, a little bit nervous.

We have a special love story. I fell in love with Deb the second I laid eyes on her. I kissed her, on a blind date, seven seconds after she walked into the room. Since that day, seven has been our favorite number.

I thought everything out to the minutest detail. I

wrote my proposal and memorized it. *Check!* I made the reservation at the restaurant overlooking the ocean. *Check!* I ordered the champagne. *Check!* In addition to knowing the date, April 7, I picked the time 7:07 p.m. I had the ring engraved with my initials, then 777, then Deb's initials. Triple 7s.

The ring was designed a month earlier, and the jeweler promised me it would be ready that Friday morning. That was cutting it a bit close since we were leaving Saturday morning for Cabo San Lucas. A few hours before my appointment to pick up the ring, I got a call from the jeweler. There was a problem, but he would do everything he could to get it done and bring it to my house that evening. I started to sweat. The most important day of my life was approaching, we were going to a foreign country, and I didn't have the ring. I was in full crisis mode.

The phone rang at 5:40 on Friday evening. With a sigh of relief, I knew it was Bob, the owner of Scorpion Jewelers. I have known him for a long time and had never had a negative service experience. Bob said, "Todd, **I've got some bad news, but before I tell you, I want you to know I have a solution.**" Bob then said, "The ring is not done. I have done everything I can, but it will not be ready until Monday. I know you are going to propose on Thursday. So, here's the plan: I just booked a flight to Cabo, and I will personally deliver the ring to you. I land on Tuesday at 1:15 p.m. We can meet somewhere, and I will have the ring for you." ***Wow!*** Talk about taking something negative and turning it all the way around into something positive. I was blown away. **My special day was saved because of a dynamic solution to a dramatic problem.** Remembering the 10 Golden Rules of Customer Service is one of the fastest ways to fix service breakdowns.

P.S. She said yes.

TEACHING MOMENT

Never deliver bad news unless you can also deliver good news. Focus on the solution, not the problem.

GOLDEN RULE
in Action

◇◇◇◇◇◇◇◇◇◇◇◇

If you can't find the time to do it right, you will never find the time to do it over.

◇◇◇◇◇◇◇◇◇◇◇◇

GOLDEN RULE

NO.

8

Offer Sizzling Guarantees

BECAUSE THIS IS so important, I am going to share two illustrations. The first involves my friend, Darren Hardy, *New York Times* bestselling author of *The Compound Effect* and *The Entrepreneur Roller Coaster*. He has a program for business professionals who are serious about success called the **High Performance Forum**. It's not cheap—about $10,000 for the year. I attended it—but only after reading his Sizzling Guarantee. Not surprisingly, he offered two.

GUARANTEE NO. 1

If, at the end of the first day of the three-day intensive workshop, you don't feel you'll get at least three times the annual membership fee in return on investment, you will be reimbursed your membership fee and given an extra $1,000 for travel expenses.

GUARANTEE NO. 2

If, at the end of the three-day intensive workshop, you don't think you will realize ten times the return of the annual membership fee in return on investment, you will be reimbursed the complete annual fee.

> ▶ **Here's the value of a sizzling guarantee: it makes providers put their money where their mouths are.**

It makes everyone step up his or her game. No business survives if they continually pay out on their guarantees. Guarantees can't be slimy or slick. They must be hard-hitting and choreographed with serious thought. Everything is on the line.

In my time with Darren, not one person exercised the guarantee. For the record, my return after the first day was not three times my return on investment; it was ten. By the end of the three days, my return was at least fifty times my investment. That is the one-two punch. By the end of one year, I made one hundred times my return on investment.

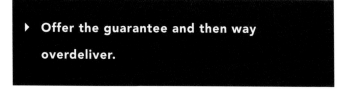

> **Offer the guarantee and then way overdeliver.**

The guarantee completely removed any risk and made doing business at a very high level comfortable for anyone who was wondering, "Was the investment worth it?" **Only people highly confident in their product make such bold guarantees. This is often the tipping point that sells the client.**

The second example involves a trip to Las Vegas. We were there to speak at a conference, and when it was all over, we wanted to celebrate the end of a multicity tour. After inquiring with the concierge and doing some internet research, we settled on a seafood restaurant that features the flair and style of famous chef Emeril Lagasse.

From the moment we arrived, we were blown away. Everything from the reception to the table to the ambience was awesome. But this place was branded as serving the best lobster in Las Vegas. Our waiter was a master of customer service. As he explained the specials, he touted the lobster as "extremely plentiful and flavorful" and that, without question, it was the best lobster in Las Vegas. Mouthwatering was what I was thinking. I asked, "How much?" He did not tell me the price. He simply said, "It will be the best money you will ever spend."

I looked at him and asked, "How much?" He didn't flinch. He said, "Mr. Duncan, it doesn't matter. It will be the best lobster you have ever had. There are 3,800 restaurants in Las Vegas, and we were voted best lobster in the entire city. I wouldn't tell you it was that good if it wasn't. You need to try this." Here comes the sizzling guarantee. He said, **"I'm so confident you will love it that if you don't, I will gladly take it back and your entire meal is on us!"** Seriously? Where's the risk? Should we order two? The rest is history. It was the best lobster we ever had. And the sizzling guarantee removed the risk.

No one ever attains success by simply doing what is required of him.

—CHARLES KENDALL ADAMS

TEACHING MOMENT

How much confidence do you have in your product? Are you willing to back it full force like Zappos, the online shoe megaretailer, which has an ironclad guarantee?

If you are not 100 percent satisfied with your purchase, you can return your order to the warehouse for a full refund. We believe that in order to have the best possible online shopping experience, our customers should not have to pay for domestic return shipping.

If, for whatever reason, you're not happy with your purchase, just go through our easy self-service return process to print out a free return label.

Our return policy is good for 365 days. If you purchased on February 29 of a leap year, then you have until February 29 of the following leap year to return those orders. That's four whole years. All we ask is to send the items back to us in their original packaging and make sure the merchandise is in the same condition.

GOLDEN RULE
in Action

✧✧✧✧✧✧✧✧✧✧✧✧

Get it right the first time, all the time,
every time.

✧✧✧✧✧✧✧✧✧✧✧✧

Recover Boldly

FOR MORE THAN twenty-one years, our company, the Duncan Group, has hosted an annual event by the name of Sales Mastery. It is our flagship event where more than two thousand of our customers come for a three-and-a-half-day transformational event on life, business, and personal productivity.

For all but about four of those years, the event has been held at the beautiful JW Marriott Desert Springs Resort & Spa in California. This sprawling property

features 833 guest rooms, fifty-four suites, three pools, and two incredible golf courses. What makes the property so exceptional is the entrance. When you walk in, you need to stop and just take it in. With an eight-story ceiling and the ambience of waterfalls, talking birds, lounges, and soft music, it feels peaceful.

This spectacular area is a core meeting place where people gather, connect, and network.

You can imagine the shock when, several years ago, the hotel was going through a major renovation and, unbeknownst to us, the entire lobby and front entrance was closed. It was completely sealed in plastic. Not only was it a disaster to look at, but also the noise from the jackhammers and workers was almost unbearable. This was a mess, and from the moment our guests began to arrive, our clients were extremely frustrated.

Bear in mind, our event is a big deal. The people who come are the best in their business. We sell out the whole hotel. Expectations are enormous! And in all the years we have hosted this event, we've never, ever had a negative experience with the hotel, until then. The problem was magnified by the fact that the Marriott had not given us any warning or even a courtesy call to expect this.

The general manager got wind of the problem and, as all great businesses do in the midst of a service

breakdown, they own the problem and the solution. **The faster you "run to customers" instead of running from them, the more likely they are to have an open mind to the solution. In fact, all great service recovery scenarios involve four things:**

▶ **a deep and sincere apology for the problem,**

▶ **a quick commitment to a solution,**

▶ **delivery of a solution that is more than expected, and**

▶ **a follow-up to make sure everything is okay.**

Our meeting with the general manager went like this:

"This is embarrassing, and on behalf of the Marriott and our property, let me say how sorry we are for this significant inconvenience. We value your business. We never want to lose you. And we want to make it up to you. I met with our team before I came over, and while we can't change the construction in the lobby, we'd like to offer your guests one free night while they are here, a free massage in our spa, and a 50 percent off coupon for any Marriott in the world for a three-night stay. Additionally, we'd like to do your event for cost and waive any of the service charges as well. How does that sound?"

This is significant. The retail value of what was offered to our guests was over $600,000. The net value to us was over $100,000 in lower costs for the event. It was, by any estimation, a brilliant recovery.

And because of the way this was handled, we signed a ten-year contract with the hotel. Every year since, the general manager welcomes us back, makes us feel special, and makes sure every step of the way they are delivering over-the-top service.

TEACHING MOMENT

When you have a breakdown, handle it fast, add massive value, give an incentive for the customer to come back, and follow up.

Customers don't expect you to be perfect. They do expect you to fix things when they go wrong.

—DONALD PORTER

GOLDEN RULE
in Action

◇◇◇◇◇◇◇◇◇◇

When you have a service breakdown, the key is how fast and how well you recover the customer. Every second counts.

◇◇◇◇◇◇◇◇◇◇

GOLDEN RULE

NO.

10

Make Saying Thank You a Big-Time Event

THE TWO MOST powerful words of influence in the service world are thank you. Too many businesses don't make the thank you a big enough deal.

I had a chance a couple of years ago to interview the great Harvey Mackay when his book *The Mackay MBA of Selling in the Real World* came out. I love interviewing superstars. When people have figured out a success equation and are passionate about their beliefs, I get really inspired to help get their message out.

I spent a day preparing for the interview. The resulting article would be distributed to more than 500,000 business professionals. I wanted to be on my game and make sure this was a solid ten.

The interview went great. Harvey and I chatted about selling for forty-five minutes. He was gracious and engaged in our conversation. We had fun. But I had no idea the lesson I was about to learn from the founder of the MackayMitchell Envelope Company— the sage of business—Mr. Harvey Mackay.

The very next morning, I was at home when FedEx delivered an overnight letter. Inside was a beautiful blue silk envelope with the Swim with the Sharks theme from Harvey's first bestselling book.

I opened the envelope and inside was a five-page letter. I was stunned. Harvey Mackay said thank you 625 times, and then, on the fifth page of the letter, he said:

MackayMitchell

Envelope Company®

Thank you! Thank you! Thank you! Thank you! Thank you!
Thank you! Thank you! Thank you! Thank you! Thank you!
Thank you! Thank you! Thank you! Thank you! Thank you!
Thank you! Thank you! Thank you! Thank you! Thank you!
Thank you! Thank you! Thank you! Thank you! Thank you!
Thank you!

Thank you! Thank you! Thank you! Thank you! Thank you!
Thank you! Thank you! Thank you! Thank you! Thank you!
Thank you! Thank you! Thank you! Thank you! Thank you!
Thank you! Thank you! Thank you! Thank you! Thank you!
Thank you! Thank you! Thank you! Thank you! Thank you!

Thank you! Thank you! Thank you! Thank you! Thank you!
Thank you! Thank you! Thank you! Thank you! Thank you!
Thank you! Thank you! Thank you! Thank you! Thank you!
Thank you! Thank you! Thank you! Thank you! Thank you!
Thank you! Thank you! Thank you! Thank you! Thank you!

I sincerely appreciate the interview and you were just awesome! The interplay between questions was spot on.

Best wishes to you for a continued year overflowing with good health, much happiness and ongoing success.

Sincerely,

Harvey Mackay

Harvey Mackay made his thank you a lasting memory. This was by far one of the best, most memorable thank-you notes I ever received in my life. I have shared this story with more than 100,000 people since I received the letter. This was the ultimate Golden Rule of Customer Service.

TEACHING MOMENT

What are the most impressive and indelible ways in which you can say thank you?

GOLDEN RULE
in Action

◇◇◇◇◇◇◇◇◇◇

The more you know about the people you serve, the better you serve the people you know.

◇◇◇◇◇◇◇◇◇◇

A Few More
GOLDEN RULES
of Customer Service

The best way to go fast is to go slow. Shortcuts could kill a customer experience.

If you don't follow up with customers, they won't follow through with you.

You will always have to do more to keep a client than you did to get a client.

A customer will not question you if you do a great job "questioning" them.

If you are not in touch with your customers, you are out of touch.

"I will take care of this for you."

No business can survive if it continually pays out on its guarantees.

You are the architect of your client's happiness.

How you serve can make or break you.

About the Authors

TODD DUNCAN

Todd is a sales entrepreneur and the visionary force behind the annual Sales Mastery Event, which impacts over sixty thousand sales professionals and millions of their clients annually.

Todd has spent his life teaching and equipping professionals with the power of high trust, the key catalyst in achieving their personal and professional dreams.

He is the author of seventeen books, including the *New York Times* bestsellers *Time Traps: Proven Strategies for Swamped Salespeople* and his groundbreaking *High Trust Selling: Make More Money in Less Time with Less Stress.*

Todd is a highly sought-after, game-changing speaker who presents solutions for the real-life challenges business professionals face daily, giving them vision, confidence, and a plan to get more out of business and life!

His mantra is: Trust yourself, your relationships, your faith, and your future. When you do that, you set in motion a universe of possibilities.

Todd has been featured in the *New York Times*, the *Wall Street Journal*, the *Los Angeles Times*, the *Seattle Times*, *Entrepreneur* magazine, *SUCCESS* magazine, the Success Network, the *Dave Ramsey Show*, and Fox News, among other media sites.

DEB DUNCAN

Deb Duncan was the founder and president of American Television Ventures. She is a pioneer in the direct response television industry. Starting while she was still in college, she was a producer of *Everybody's Money Matters* on the Lifetime Television Network. She has written, produced, and directed more than one hundred direct response TV programs. She has great insights on how to frame your message, make powerful promises, and get people to respond.

Deb is the author of two children's fairy tales, *A Thousand Princes* and *Mrs. Prince*, as well as several screenplays. She is the coauthor of *5 Stars: Building High Ratings and High Trust in the Digital Age* and *The 10 Golden Rules of Customer Service* along with her fabulous husband, Todd Duncan.